W9-BYE-465

SMOKING AND HEALTH

LIFE GUIDES

SMOKING AND HEALTH

Brian R. Ward

Series consultant:
Dr Alan Maryon-Davis
MB BChir. MSc MRCP FFCM

LIFE GUIDES

Franklin Watts

London · New York · Sydney · Toronto

© 1986 Franklin Watts

First published in 1986 by
Franklin Watts
12a Golden Square
London W1

First published in the USA by
Franklin Watts Inc.
387 Park Avenue South
New York, N. Y. 10016

First published in Australia by
Franklin Watts Australia
14 Mars Road
Lane Cove, NSW 2066

UK edition: ISBN 0 86313 4017
US edition: ISBN 0-531-10180-0
Library of Congress Catalog Card No: 0-85-52043

Design: Howard Dyke

Picture research: Anne-Marie Ehrlich

Illustrations:
John Bavosi, Dick Bonson, Penny Dann, Howard Dyke
Rose Eddington, Sally Launder, Annie Owen.

Photographs:
Compix 22
E. T. Archive Ltd 19*b*
Sally and Richard Greenhill 30
Robert Harding 23
Health Education Council 7*r*, 32, 41
Hutchison Library 20*b*, 21*tl*, 21*tr*, 45
London Chest Hospital 11
NAAS 44
Peter Newarks' Western Americana 18, 19*t*
Radio Times Hulton Picture Library 20*t*
Sporting Pictures Ltd 6, 43
John Watney 29   ZEFA 7*l*, 21*b*, 27

Printed in Belgium

Contents

Introduction

By displaying cigarette brand names prominently, many sponsors of sporting events promote a glamorous image of smoking. In this way the cigarette companies try to overcome the recent move away from cigarettes on health grounds.

Why do people smoke? Why do they take up a habit which other people find unpleasant? Why start a habit which is hard to break?

Most young people try their first cigarette when it is offered to them by a friend. Sometimes they are afraid to refuse in case their friends make fun of them. So they accept the cigarette, in spite of the unpleasant taste. If your friends all smoke, it may at first seem difficult to be the odd one out.

Until quite recently the majority of adults smoked, and it was even regarded as a fashionable habit. But this was before the publication of a number of health reports which showed quite clearly that smoking is the cause of many serious diseases.

Now the number of adult smokers is dropping steadily, but young people are still taking up the habit. Although statistics show that about 320,000 people die in the USA each year from smoking-related diseases, some young people don't believe this will ever happen to them. So it is important to understand the risks of smoking and to see how tobacco smoke affects the body.

Many children start to smoke by copying their parents' habits. Adults often do not realize how easily their children can be influenced.

Smoking as an addiction

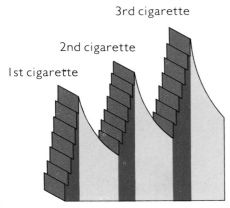

3rd cigarette

2nd cigarette

1st cigarette

With each puff of a cigarette, a smoker takes in a small but measurable amount of nicotine. This gradually builds up in the blood and is only slowly removed from it. So the effects of the next cigarette are added to the first, and the blood level of nicotine rises with each new cigarette smoked.

There are no doubts about the health problems and risks to life caused by smoking, so why do people take up the habit?

Some young people start smoking because they think it will make them look or feel more mature. They may simply be copying their parents or older brothers and sisters. And once they have picked up the habit, they become addicted. They come to depend on smoking to help them through the ups and downs of their daily life, to help them relax or stay alert, or simply to relieve boredom.

When a smoker inhales a cigarette, a substance called **nicotine** is absorbed into the blood. It is carried to the brain in just a few seconds. Nicotine is an addictive drug – it produces chemical changes in the brain which cause a craving for nicotine. It also creates unpleasant sensations as the effects wear off. These are called **withdrawal symptoms**.

Smoking also produces another type of addiction – the "habit." Smokers come to depend on the small rituals they develop. The tapping of a cigarette on the back of the hand, flicking off ash unnecessarily, and patting the pockets to find matches are all smoking rituals. Some people find these little rituals just as difficult to do without as the physical effect of the nicotine.

The effects of a cigarette can be felt in a very short time. This graph shows how nicotine is absorbed very rapidly. It reaches the brain in a few seconds and affects other parts of the body in just a few minutes.

Nicotine level in the blood

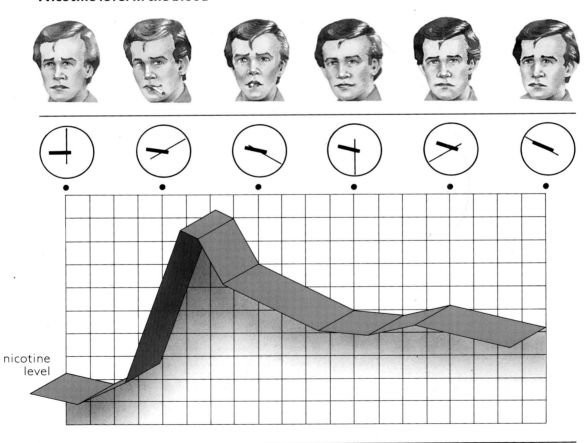

nicotine level

How tobacco smoke affects the body

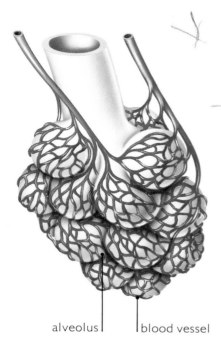

alveolus | blood vessel

The chemicals in smoke are absorbed in the lungs through the walls of tiny air sacs called **alveoli**. Their proper function is to absorb the oxygen we need in order to live. The walls of alveoli are covered with tiny blood vessels, or **capillaries**, which carry away the absorbed substances.

When tobacco burns, it produces **tar,** nicotine, and a mixture of many other chemicals and gases. All of these are inhaled into the **lungs**.

Nicotine is the substance which gives smokers the enjoyable "lift." The effects of nicotine are complicated.

Most smokers feel that nicotine makes them feel relaxed. But nicotine actually increases the heart rate and blood pressure and causes the stomach to produce extra acid. Some of its effects increase the risk of serious disease.

Carbon monoxide is a colorless gas which is quickly absorbed in the lungs. It becomes chemically attached to **hemoglobin**, the red substance in our blood which carries life-giving **oxygen** around the body. By doing this it reduces the amount of oxygen the blood cells can carry, starving the tissues of this vital substance.

The other important material in tobacco smoke is tar, the brown sticky residue which leaves dark marks on the fingers and teeth of habitual smokers. Tar has very damaging effects on the lungs and is the cause of smokers' cough and more serious disease.

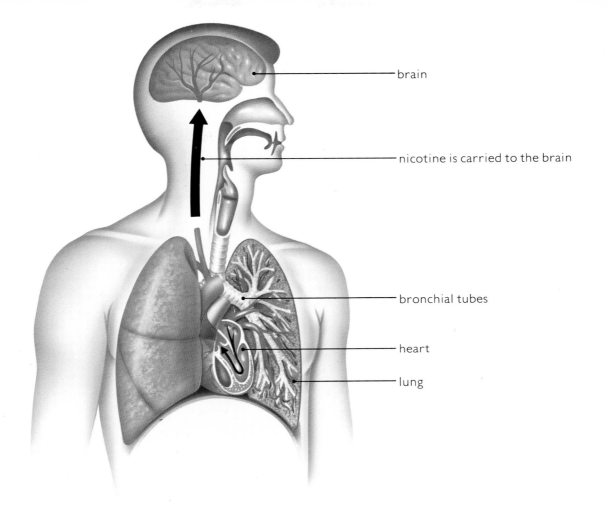

brain

nicotine is carried to the brain

bronchial tubes

heart

lung

△ When tobacco smoke is inhaled, tar is deposited in the lungs. Nicotine is absorbed through the lungs and is carried to the brain in the bloodstream. Carbon monoxide also enters the blood and is carried around the body. This gas is thought to be one of the causes of heart disease and circulation disorders in smokers.

Shown in cross-section, a normal lung (left) is a healthy pink color. But the smoker's lung (right) is discolored by tar. The large pale patch is caused by lung cancer.

Smoking and the lungs

1 In bronchitis the tubes leading to the alveoli become inflamed.

2 The alveoli of heavy smokers may become enlarged and thickened. This condition is called emphysema.

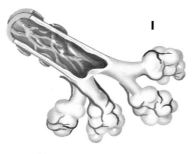

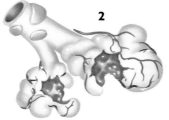

Although tobacco has always been suspected of causing health problems, it is only in the last twenty years that enough evidence has been gathered to show that it is a killer. **Lung cancer** is twenty-five times more common in smokers than in people who have never smoked. And the younger people are when they start to smoke, the greater is the risk of developing cancer later in life.

It is thought that lung cancer is caused by irritant chemicals from tar remaining in contact with lung tissues for so long that the cells become cancerous.

Much more common than lung cancer is **bronchitis**, a serious inflammation of the tubes leading into the lungs. These can become blocked by jelly-like **mucus**, and the damaged tissue is then easily infected by bacteria. Bronchitis can also affect non-smokers, but it is much more common and much worse in smokers.

Emphysema is another disease which affects heavy smokers. The lung tissue breaks down as a result of the constant irritation and cannot absorb oxygen properly. At least 90 per cent of the deaths from bronchitis and emphysema occur among smokers.

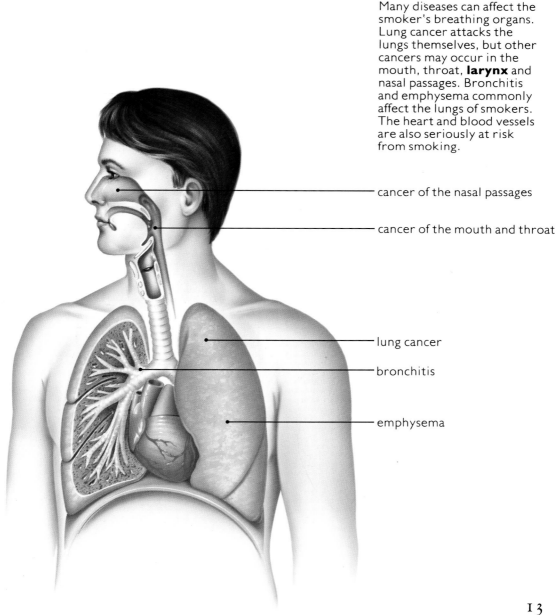

Many diseases can affect the smoker's breathing organs. Lung cancer attacks the lungs themselves, but other cancers may occur in the mouth, throat, **larynx** and nasal passages. Bronchitis and emphysema commonly affect the lungs of smokers. The heart and blood vessels are also seriously at risk from smoking.

cancer of the nasal passages

cancer of the mouth and throat

lung cancer

bronchitis

emphysema

Smoking and the heart

Smoking cigarettes has been shown to be responsible for some very dangerous diseases of the heart and the circulation.

It is not certain which of the substances in tobacco smoke cause the bad effects on the heart, but nicotine and carbon monoxide are probably the most important. One effect of smoking on the blood is to increase the amounts of fatty substances it contains. (This causes the blood to become more viscous, or thicker, so the heart has to work harder to push it around the body, and through the very narrow capillaries.) Smoking also increases the tendency of the blood to clot.

This chart shows the unnecessary deaths caused by smoking. As you can see, heart disease and other diseases of the blood circulation are the most common.

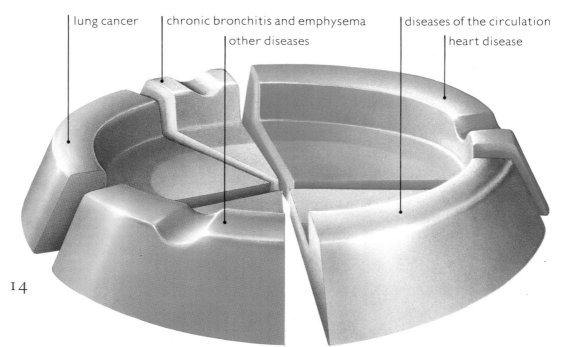

lung cancer   chronic bronchitis and emphysema   diseases of the circulation

other diseases   heart disease

People who don't smoke
have a much better chance of
living to enjoy their
retirement. And they are
less likely to suffer other
illnesses such as bronchitis,
which can make life a misery
for the elderly.

Eventually, the fatty materials can be deposited on the walls of blood vessels, gradually narrowing them and causing obstructions to the blood flow. If the blood supply to the heart tissue itself becomes blocked in this way, the heart becomes damaged and works less efficiently. The blood can even become blocked off completely so part of the heart dies, in a heart attack.

Smokers are on average about three times more likely to have a heart attack than non-smokers. Men who smoke are even more likely to develop obstructed **arteries** in the legs and elsewhere.

1 The arteries of smokers may be suddenly blocked by blood clots.

2 The smoker's arteries may gradually become blocked by deposits called **atheroma**.

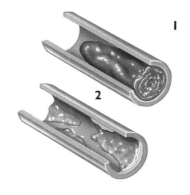

How serious is the problem?

Researchers have come up with some frightening figures to show just how dangerous the smoking habit is. This has meant studying millions of people throughout the world over many years.

If you smoked twenty cigarettes a day, your life would be shortened by about five years. This means that, for every cigarette you smoke, you are losing about five minutes from your life.

Another way to look at the risk is to reckon that for every thousand young adults who smoke regularly:
1 will be murdered
6 will be killed in road accidents
250 will die because of smoking
before the age of 65.

Most smokers will tell you that they know an old person who has smoked all his or her life and appears to be healthy. Some people probably are less liable to be affected by the diseases usually caused by smoking. But when the health records of thousands of people are examined in detail over many years, there is no doubt about the risk for the average person. In the United States approximately 320,000 people die prematurely each year because of smoking.

murder victims

road accident victims

smokers dying before the age of 65

There is no doubt that smoking is a serious risk to life as well as health. If you are a regular smoker, you are 250 times more likely to be killed by its effects before you are 65 than you are to be murdered! And smoking is 40 times more likely to cause your early death than a road accident. With these odds, it doesn't seem worth the gamble of smoking.

The introduction of tobacco

America is the natural home of tobacco, and smoking was part of a tribal ritual among North American Indians.

No one knows when the practice of smoking the dried leaves of the tobacco plant first began, but it is certain that the ancient Maya and Aztec Indians of Central America smoked tobacco. The early Spanish explorers reported that the Indians smoked or chewed the weed, and the plant was soon introduced into Europe. During the sixteeth century tobacco in various forms was used medicinally, although its use for smoking enjoyment was discouraged by doctors. Before the end of the seventeenth century smoking had spread throughout most of the world.

Adventurers like Drake and Raleigh popularized smoking and snuff-taking in Europe, while others began a fierce battle against the habit. King James I of England campaigned against tobacco, and in many countries laws were passed against smoking. However, these attacks died out when it was realized that huge amounts of money could be raised by taxing the growing tobacco trade.

In the Spanish territories around the Caribbean and in the British colonies in Virginia tobacco was grown and exported to Europe.

△ Tobacco was cultivated in
North America to supply the
demands from Europe.
Tobacco plantations were set
up, leading to the
development of the slave
trade. Large fleets of sailing
ships carried the crop to
Europe.

▷ Once introduced into
Europe, the smoking habit
became very popular.
Because tobacco was at first
very expensive, its use was
restricted to wealthier
people.

The spread of the smoking habit

Originally tobacco was consumed in the form of pipe tobacco, cigars, chewing tobacco and snuff (a powdered form of tobacco). Cigarettes were invented in Brazil and first used in the Latin countries. They did not become really popular in the rest of Europe until the end of the nineteenth century.

At first cigarettes were hand-rolled, but soon the habit spread to the United States, where automatic cigarette-rolling machines were introduced. From then on smoking spread very rapidly. Between 1895 and 1909 twelve American states banned smoking, but these laws were ignored.

△ Cigarette smoking increased in popularity during World War I, both on the fighting front and in the war factories.

▷ The use of modern cigarettes has even spread to the wilder parts of the world, such as the South American jungles.

△ In some parts of the world a pipe is part of the traditional dress worn to distinguish one tribe from its neighbors. These men are Dinka warriors from the Sudan.

▷ Many countries have traditional ways to use tobacco. This South American boy is using a pipe; many of his fellow Indians use snuff or chew tobacco.

Smoking has always been more popular among men than women. In most countries about a third to half of all adult men smoke, and in the Third World usually only a low proportion of women are smokers. In Europe and North America it was not until after World War I that women took up the habit. During World War II many women working in factories began to smoke heavily, and the number of women smokers continued to rise.

Many developed nations and Third World countries now earn so much money from the tobacco trade that they become dependent on the revenue. They cannot afford to ban smoking, in spite of the health risks.

▽ Cigars are an expensive luxury for most smokers. They are made by rolling a large tobacco leaf around the specially treated tobacco.

Tobacco cultivation and processing

Nicotiana

▽ Tobacco growing is very big business, and in many tropical and sub-tropical parts of the world there are large plantations where it is cultivated.

There are many varieties of the tobacco plant, which has the Latin name *Nicotiana*. It is a relative of the Petunia and is often grown in the garden as a decorative plant.

Tobacco is a valuable crop which can be grown in a range of climates from the tropics to Northern Europe and North America. The plants are grown outdoors and develop rapidly to a height of 2–3m (6–9 ft). When the leaves are ripe, they are picked, packed into bunches, and hung up to dry. Most tobacco is cured by being blasted with hot air. It is then shredded to make pipe, cigar, or cigarette tobacco.

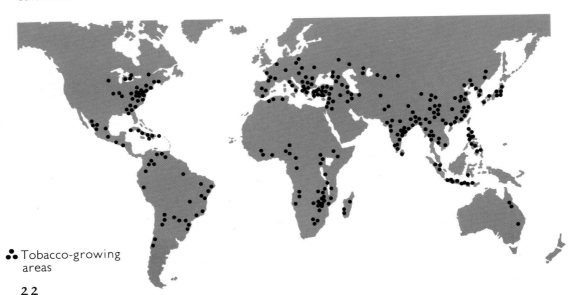

•• Tobacco-growing areas

◁ Large cigars are made almost entirely by hand, which is the main reason for their high price.

▽ Tobacco cultivation uses large areas of fertile land and requires many workers to tend and harvest it.

△ Although tobacco production is highly mechanized, it requires skillful manual work to grade the shredded tobacco before it is made into cigarettes.

There are many types of tobacco products. Some countries traditionally prefer very strong, dark tobacco, while others use light, mild tobacco. Chewing tobacco and snuff are popular in many Third World markets.

Most countries in the warmer parts of the world grow tobacco for their own use, but for others it is a very important export crop. Major tobacco producers include Zimbabwe, the United States, the Soviet Union, Pakistan, Brazil and Central America.

23

Tobacco in all its forms

In general, the risks from smoking depend on the amount inhaled and the type of tobacco. Cigarette smokers inhale deeply, absorbing most of the nicotine and carbon monoxide in the smoke and depositing tar in their lungs. Cigar and pipe smokers do not usually inhale so much, and have only a slightly greater risk of an early death than non-smokers. But they are more likely to suffer from cancer of the mouth, nose and throat than non-smokers.

As people become more aware of the risks, forms of tobacco mouth wads are

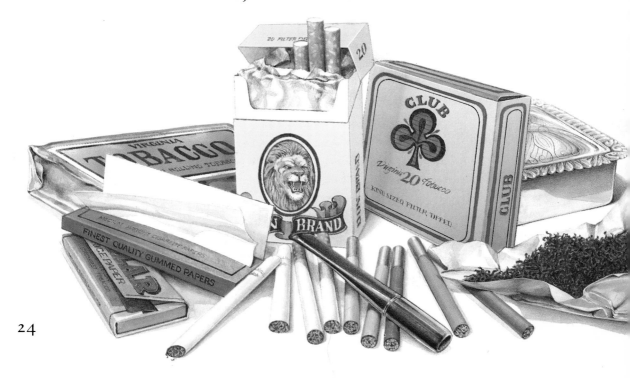

being introduced in some countries in an attempt to make up for the falling demand for cigarettes. These new tobacco wads have not yet been properly investigated. No one knows what health problems will follow the use of these new forms of tobacco, or of snuff taking, but cancers of the mouth and nose can be expected to increase if the habit becomes common.

There is no really safe way to take tobacco. By switching from one type of tobacco product to another, a different set of risks arises.

Tobacco comes in a wide variety of forms. All of them are harmful to health. Smoking affects the heart, circulation and lungs, but chewing or sucking tobacco and snuff can cause cancer of the mouth and lips.

Reducing the risk?

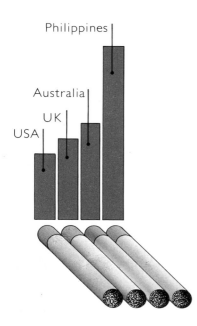

International brands of cigarettes may all look the same, but they are maufactured with different amounts of tar and nicotine to suit tastes in particular countries. Some contain dangerously high levels of tar.

There have been many attempts to reduce the harmful effects of cigarette smoking, while keeping the "enjoyable" effects of nicotine. Smokers inhale to obtain the amount of nicotine they need to produce the effect they desire. So if they smoke mild cigarettes, low in nicotine, they tend to smoke more of them to maintain their nicotine intake. If they smoke very strong cigarettes, fewer will be needed.

Unfortunately, cigarettes contain the cancer-forming tar in similar proportions to the nicotine. Although health authorities recommend low-tar cigarettes to reduce the risks of smoking, most smokers simply smoke more of them to keep up their nicotine intake.

Filters are intended to remove tar, but they have not proved very effective. Tar particles are so fine that it is almost impossible to remove them while still allowing nicotine fumes to pass though the filter material.

One recent attempt to reduce the dangers of smoking was the introduction of a synthetic smoking material. This was not accepted by smokers, and is no longer generally available.

Herbal tobacco and even cannabis have been used as tobacco substitutes in an attempt to avoid the risks of nicotine. But any herbal material will produce a large number of potentially dangerous substances when burned, including tar and carbon monoxide. The risks they carry are therefore likely to be just as great.

The tar content of cigarette smoke is measured on an artificial smoking machine. Manufacturers and health researchers use such machines to study cigarettes and the effects of their smoke.

The costs to the community

Smoking is a major health problem, causing misery to those affected by smoking-related diseases, but its costs are enormous in other ways.

Millions of working days are lost each year because of absences caused by smoker's diseases. Workers who smoke more than twenty cigarettes each day have to take at least twice as much time off work because of illness than do non-smokers.

The other costs to the community are just as great. Many of the diseases which can be caused by smoking, such as bronchitis and emphysema, require long periods of medical and nursing care, which are very expensive. In addition there are the social security and insurance payments which have to be made to the sufferers or their relatives.

Smoking is also directly expensive to the smoker. Especially in the Third World, the cost of tobacco may form a large part of the smoker's income – money which could be better spent on food and housing. If smokers become ill, they lose money because they are unable to work, and they may suffer premature retirement or early death.

Opposite

Many lung conditions associated with smoking involve lengthy and expensive medical and nursing care. Hospital beds are therefore occupied by patients who could have avoided ill health.

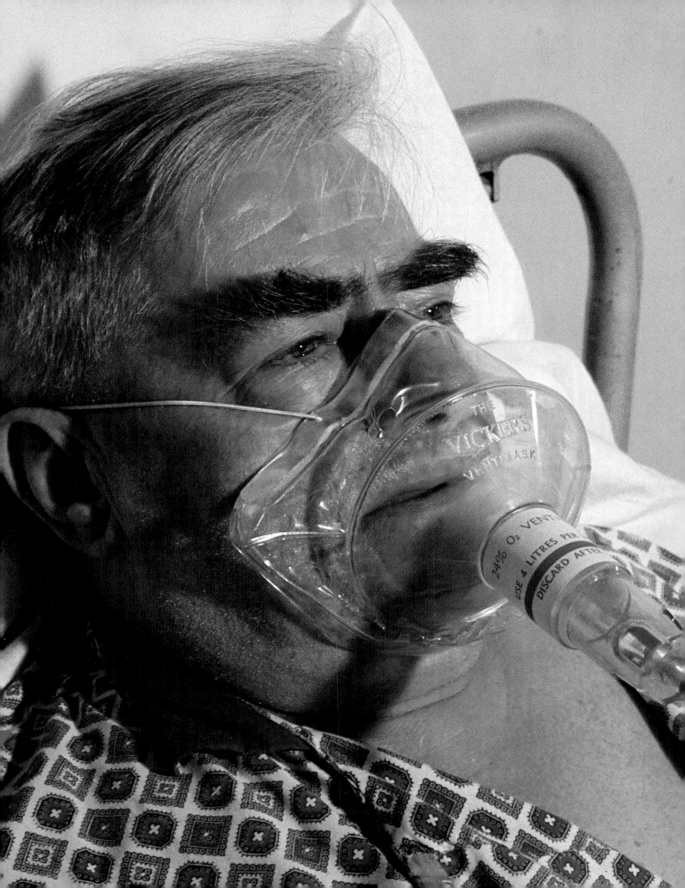

Breathing other people's smoke

When a cigarette is inhaled, the smoker filters most of the dangerous substances from the smoke before blowing it out again. But smoke is also released directly into the air from the cigarette when the smoker is not inhaling. It is this "sidestream" smoke which is of concern to non-smokers.

This sidestream smoke is a health hazard, as it contains far more chemical irritants than the smoke exhaled by the smoker. Because cigar and pipe smokers tend not to inhale their smoke, the effects on non-smokers are even worse.

It has been found that people who work or live with smokers may actually develop the same sort of lung damage as the smokers themselves, although not as badly.

For people already suffering from bronchitis or **asthma**, passive exposure to cigarette smoke is not only unpleasant; it may make their condition worse.

Quite apart from the health risks, many non-smokers find cigarette smoke very uncomfortable. It can irritate the eyes, nose and throat and the smell of stale tobacco lingers in clothes and hair.

The passive smoker has no choice about the cigarette smoke inhaled. To the non-smoker cigarette smoke is both a nuisance and a health hazard. Not surprisingly, non-smokers are becoming less willing to tolerate smoke, expecially in public places.

The "sidestream" smoke given off from an unattended cigarette or pipe contains large amounts of irritant chemicals.

Tobacco and the child

Health authorities try to ensure that mothers-to-be are aware of the dangers of smoking in pregnancy.

Young children in the families of smokers are exposed to the same hazards as other passive smokers. They have twice the risk of serious chest illnesses if both parents smoke than if neither does.

But the greatest dangers to the child begin even before it is born. If the mother smokes during pregnancy, her baby is more likely to be smaller than normal. The more she smokes, the smaller her baby is likely to be. This is probably because some of the substances she inhales from smoke are passed in her blood to the developing baby. These are poisons, which affect the baby more than an adult.

The mother who smokes during pregnancy is more likely to lose her unborn baby because of a miscarriage than if she doesn't smoke. But even after the baby is born, if it is small and premature, it is much more likely to have early health problems than the normal weight babies of non-smokers.

If the mother continues to smoke, the risk continues. Her baby is exposed to tobacco smoke, and if it is breast fed, it will also take in nicotine with the mother's milk. Right up to the age of ten

If the mother continues to smoke after her baby is born, it will be exposed to harmful sidestream smoke. If she breast feeds her child, it will take in nicotine with her milk.

or eleven years, the children of mothers who smoked throughout their pregnancy continue to be slightly smaller than the average child.

But probably the worst effects are in the example set to the child. Research has shown that children who grow up in a home where the parents smoke are far more likely to become smokers themselves when they grow up. Some parents even introduce their children to smoking, setting a bad example that may take years to overcome.

The special risks for women

Until recent years women seemed to
suffer less from smoker's diseases. Then
as the numbers of women smokers began
to rise, diseases like lung cancer,
bronchitis and heart attacks increased to
almost the same levels as in men. In the
United States, over the past ten years,
lung cancer rates in women have
increased by more than 90 per cent, and
the figure is still rising.

But smoking has some special risks for
women. Women who smoke find it less
easy to become pregnant, and they
remain fertile for a slightly shorter time.

Because women have
followed men into the
smoking habit, they are
experiencing the same
health problems that have
been affecting male smokers.

34

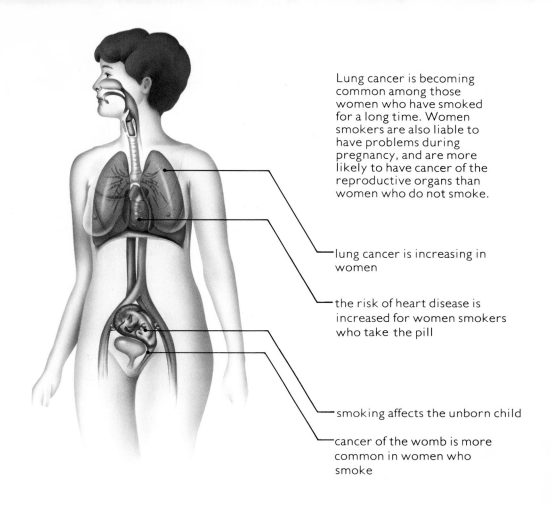

Lung cancer is becoming common among those women who have smoked for a long time. Women smokers are also liable to have problems during pregnancy, and are more likely to have cancer of the reproductive organs than women who do not smoke.

lung cancer is increasing in women

the risk of heart disease is increased for women smokers who take the pill

smoking affects the unborn child

cancer of the womb is more common in women who smoke

When they do become pregnant, the risks which may affect their unborn child can also present a health hazard for the mother.

Women smokers who take the contraceptive pill are at special risk, as they have a much greater chance of suffering from heart attacks, strokes, and other diseases of the blood circulation. These risks increase dramatically for women over the age of about thirty-five. Cancer of the womb is also more common among women smokers, as are a number of other serious diseases.

Giving up

Cold turkey: the simplest method is to stop completely, and without cheating. It needs a lot of willpower, as the smoker will probably suffer from nicotine withdrawal effects.

You will probably be sensible enough never to start smoking, but you may know someone who has, and who wants to give up. It won't be easy. But many people have successfully managed to give up, and in the United States there are about 37 million ex-smokers.

Because smoking is a real addiction, and not just a comfortable habit, some people find it very difficult to stop. It is

Reduction: people with plenty of willpower can sometimes reduce their cigarette consumption gradually before stopping. But the temptation is to creep back up again to the previous level of smoking.

Low tar: simply switching from high- or medium-tar cigarettes to a low-tar brand cuts the intake of the dangerous substances in smoke. But most smokers consume more of these less-satisfying cigarettes, so the risk is not reduced.

Medical care: many doctors will help their patients to stop smoking by providing advice and treatment.

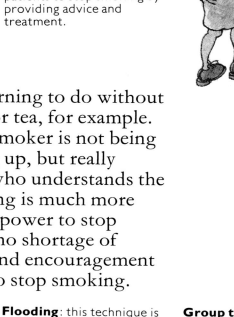

much harder than learning to do without sugar in your coffee or tea, for example. It is much easier if a smoker is not being pressured into giving up, but really wants to. A smoker who understands the health risks of smoking is much more likely to have the willpower to stop completely. There is no shortage of helpful information and encouragement for anyone wanting to stop smoking.

Flooding: this technique is sometimes successful in sickening a person of smoking. They simply smoke one cigarette after another until they feel thoroughly ill, then repeat the process until they cannot face another cigarette.

Group therapy: for the really hardened smoker, there are special clinics where the problem can be treated with long sessions of therapy.

37

Return to health

When a smoker gives up the habit, the positive benefits start right away. Nicotine and carbon monoxide levels in the blood are reduced. However, the ex-smoker may at first feel restless and irritable and unable to concentrate. All these are typical withdrawal symptoms from the addictive drug nicotine. But these side effects are only temporary, and the body soon adjusts itself.

Without the constant flow of tar and other irritants, the normal cleansing process in the lungs gradually starts to work again. The tiny beating hairs in the air passages begin to pump mucus and accumulated dirt back out of the lungs. For a while the ex-smoker may actually cough more than ever, as the cleansing action gets started.

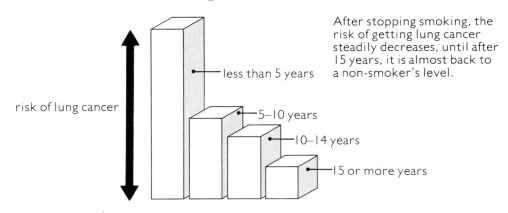

risk of lung cancer

less than 5 years

5–10 years

10–14 years

15 or more years

After stopping smoking, the risk of getting lung cancer steadily decreases, until after 15 years, it is almost back to a non-smoker's level.

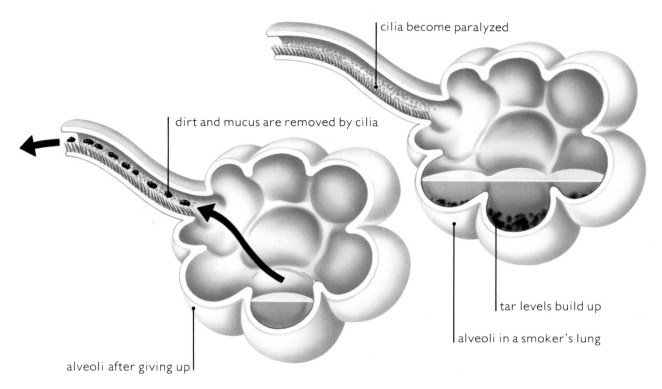

cilia become paralyzed

dirt and mucus are removed by cilia

tar levels build up

alveoli in a smoker's lung

alveoli after giving up

Gradually, however, breathing becomes easier and the lungs work more efficiently. After a while the senses of smell and taste, which are affected by smoking, will return to normal, and the ex-smoker finds that food tastes better.

Year by year the risk of dying from lung cancer or a heart attack becomes smaller, until after ten to fifteen years the ex-smoker is at little more risk than a person who has never smoked.

Tar collects in the lungs when the normal cleaning process ceases to work. Dirt inhaled into the alveoli is normally trapped in a layer of sticky mucus, which is carried out of the lungs by currents produced by tiny beating hairs. These hairs, or **cilia**, are paralyzed by tar, so cleaning does not take place effectively. When a person stops smoking, the cilia begin to beat again, and the dirt and mucus is removed.

Changing attitudes

In most countries in the West the number of smokers is falling. Smoking is no longer seen to be an acceptable habit. Today smokers are in the minority and non-smokers outnumber smokers by two to one.

Why have our attitudes to smoking changed? The risks of smoking are now well established, and even the most hardened smoker knows about the danger of lung cancer. Fewer people are aware of the association with heart disease and bronchitis, but health education is helping to change this.

Anti-smoking campaigns have been launched in schools throughout the country to make young people aware of the facts about smoking. Each year the government spends large sums of money to support anti-smoking advertisements on television and in newspapers.

Because of these changing attitudes it has become possible to restrict the places in which people are allowed to smoke. Smoking is banned in most grocery stores, in many theaters and in most hospitals and school buildings. No-smoking areas are designated on many trains, buses and planes.

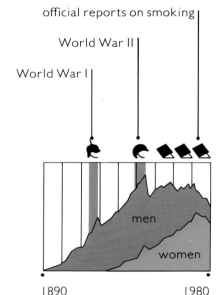

official reports on smoking

World War II

World War I

men

women

1890   1980

Tobacco consumption steadily increased during the first part of this century, especially during the two world wars. When official reports on the dangers of smoking were published, many men gave up, although the habit continued to rise for a while among women.

40

No wonder smokers cough.

The tar and discharge that collects in [...] of an average smoker.

The Health Education Council
Helping you to better health

All around the world public health authorities and other organizations produce literature and posters to help educate people about the risks of smoking.

WHY NICK O'TEEN IS A WEED.

CIGARETTES LEAVE STAINS ON HIS TEETH, MAKE HIS BREATH SMELL AND HIS CLOTHES STINK.

HE CAN'T ESCAPE ME. HE SMOKES SO MUCH HE PUFFS AND PANTS LIKE A BROKEN DOWN STEAM ENGINE.

NICK O'TEEN IS A WRECK. IF HE HAD X-RAY VISION LIKE ME, HE COULD SEE THE DAMAGE CIGARETTES DO TO HIS HEART AND LUNGS.

The Health Education Council
Helping you to better health

The right to choose

Do we have the right to tell people how they may enjoy themselves? Should smoking be banned altogether to protect people from its effects? No government has yet solved this problem. Governments must decide whether they can afford to do without the tax raised from smokers and to risk losing the votes of millions of smokers if they were to ban the practice.

What they can do is to discourage smoking gradually by putting strict controls on advertising. Cigarette advertisements are now banned on television and radio, and those that appear on posters or in newspapers must carry a health warning. By law every cigarette pack must also carry a warning about the risks of smoking, and it is illegal to sell cigarettes to children under the age of eighteen.

Governments are less willing to interfere with what people do in the privacy of their own homes. It seems that adults are now aware of the risks they face from smoking, but young people may still need some legal protection as long as they continue to experiment with smoking.

Opposite

The big international tobacco companies have been fighting back against restrictions on advertising by sponsoring sporting events. This enables them to promote their product and associate it with a glamorous or healthy pastime.

The moral problem

Smoking *is* a moral problem, quite apart from the economic arguments for and against tobacco. In the countries where tobacco is used and processed, thousands of people are employed in making or selling tobacco products. But it has been estimated that in Western countries the price for every job in the tobacco manufacturing industry is the death of five smokers each year.

This farmer in Bangladesh can earn far more by selling a tobacco crop than by growing cereals. This is why tobacco is grown in many poorer countries which are unable to feed themselves.

Despite the famine in the Sudan, this Dinka villager is using scarce water resources to tend his tobacco crop rather than growing food to eat.

More than half of the world's tobacco is grown by poor or developing nations, who desperately need the cash this crop brings. But to grow the crop, they use their best agricultural land.

In the developed countries cigarette sales are falling, so the tobacco manufacturers are trying to sell more in the Third World. These countries already have problems in feeding their own people. And in years to come, on top of malnutrition, they can expect an epidemic of all the smoker's diseases we have been experiencing in the West.

Glossary

Alveoli: tiny air sacs in the lungs in which oxygen is absorbed from the air. Alveoli are easily damaged by smoking or by air pollution.

Artery: blood vessel carrying blood away from the heart. Its walls are thick and muscular.

Nicotiana

Asthma: illness caused by narrowing of the small air passages in the lungs, making it difficult to breathe. Asthma is thought to be a type of allergy.

Atheroma: fatty deposit on the wall of an artery. It builds up and can interfere with the blood flow. If a blood clot (thrombosis) forms on it, the artery can become completely blocked.

Bronchial tubes: large tubes conveying air into the lungs.

Bronchitis: inflammation of the walls of the bronchial tubes. Bronchitis is very common among smokers and people breathing polluted air.

Capillaries: the narrowest blood vessels through which blood passes before being returned to the heart along the veins. Oxygen can pass from the blood through the capillary walls.

Carbon monoxide: A colorless, poisonous gas which is produced when tobacco burns. It interferes with the blood's ability to carry oxygen.

Cilia: tiny beating hairs lining the air passages which play an important part in keeping the lungs clean. They help remove dirt particles trapped in a layer of mucus. Tobacco smoke paralyzes the cilia, allowing tar to accumulate in the lungs.

Emphysema: lung disease in which the alveoli become enlarged and thickened so that they no longer absorb oxygen efficiently. The disease is common among smokers.

Hemoglobin: the red substance in the blood which allows it to absorb and carry oxygen around the body.

Larynx: the "voice box," a tough box-like structure in the throat. Cancer of the larynx can affect smokers.

Lungs: paired spongy organs in the chest with which we breathe. The delicate lungs are affected by tobacco smoke.

Lung cancer: very serious disease common among smokers. It affects the bronchial tubes and the lung tissue itself and is difficult to treat. The disease is very uncommon in people who have never smoked.

Mucus: sticky liquid lining the lungs and air passages. It traps dirt and moistens the lung surface so that oxygen can be absorbed.

Nicotine: poisonous drug found in tobacco which causes addiction to smoking.

Oxygen: transparent gas present in the air we breathe which is essential for life.

Tar: dark, sticky liquid, containing many irritant chemicals, which is produced by burning tobacco. Tar deposited in the lungs is thought to be responsible for lung cancer in smokers.

Withdrawal symptoms: the unpleasant effects of giving up smoking in a person who has become addicted to nicotine. They can include sickness, shaking, headaches and many other unpleasant feelings. However these side effects are only temporary and gradually wear off.

Index

PRINTED IN BELGIUM BY
proost
INTERNATIONAL BOOK PRODUCTION